ON THE ROAD AGAIN!

ENJOY THE JOURNEY!

We've simplified cooking on the road! You'll find complete menus for five 3-day trips *(breakfast, lunch, and dinner each day, plus snacks and desserts)* and a grocery list for each adventure.

Meal plans use leftovers in smart new ways so you won't waste food or drag uneaten items back home. Recipes tell you when to prep food ahead or reserve food for a later meal.

All recipes make four servings and can be cooked outside on a campfire or inside your RV using a stovetop or oven. Use a cooler or camper fridge to keep food cold.

ISBN-13: 978-1-56383-611-4
Item #2918

Printed in the USA by G&R Publishing Co.

Distributed By:

507 Industrial Street
Waverly, IA 50677

www.cqbookstore.com

gifts@cqbookstore.com

 CQ Products

 CQ Products

 @cqproducts

 @cqproducts

HERE'S HOW

1. Look at each Menu at a Glance and choose a trip meal plan you like.

2. Stock your RV with the staples and supplies you'll need (see the list below).

3. Use the trip's Shopping List to buy your groceries and any remaining staples or supplies, and purchase other beverages, snacks, or convenience items you want.

4. If you'd like, prep some foods at h̶ ̶ ̶ ̶ ̶ ̶ ̶ ̶m for transporting (see ideas below).

5. Hit the road!

STAPLES & SUP

- **Seasonings:** salt, black pe̶ ̶ ̶ ̶ ̶alt & powder, onion powder, minced garli̶ ̶ ̶ ̶ka, cinnamon, cinnamon-sugar, and other seasonings you like to use

- **Baking supplies:** flour, sugar, brown sugar, baking powder, nonfat dry milk, honey, and vanilla (not everything is used on every trip)

- Cooking spray and oils (vegetable, olive, and/or coconut oil)

- Heavy-duty foil and disposable 9 x 9" foil pans

- Hot pads, long tongs, skewers, campfire forks/sticks, and cast iron cookware (refer to recipes)

BEFORE YOU LEAVE HOME

- Wash, cut, and pack vegetables that won't turn brown.

- Premeasure and mix dry ingredients for baking.

- Bake any take-along items, like muffins (page 33).

Day 1

Avocado Breakfast Boats
Sweet Tortilla Roll-Ups

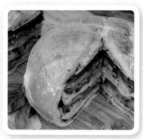

Make-Ahead Picnic Loaf

Meatball Stew Packs
Garlic Biscuits

Day 2

Breakfast Burgers
Apple Wedges

Aloha Quesadillas

Walking Tacos
Dessert Cups

Day 3

Blueberry Cinnamon Rolls
Fireside Granola

Loaded Baked Potatoes
Garden Salad

Spaghetti & Meatballs
Veggie Platter & S'mores Cups

TRIP 1 *Shopping List*

Dairy

- [ ] 1 stick butter
- [ ] 4 slices Colby Jack cheese
- [ ] 2 C. shredded Monterey Jack cheese
- [ ] 5 to 6 oz. swiss cheese slices
- [ ] 2⅓ C. milk
- [ ] 1 can grated Parmesan cheese
- [ ] 8 oz. sour cream, optional

Fresh Fruits & Veggies

- [ ] 2 small zucchini
- [ ] 1 (16 oz.) pkg. mini bell peppers
- [ ] 1 large yellow onion
- [ ] 1 pt. grape tomatoes
- [ ] 1 red apple
- [ ] 1 pt. blueberries
- [ ] 2 avocados
- [ ] 1 small head cabbage
- [ ] 1 bag spinach or lettuce
- [ ] 1 lemon
- [ ] 4 large russet potatoes
- [ ] 8 oz. sliced mushrooms
- [ ] 1 bunch asparagus

Breads & Grains

- [ ] 12 (6") flour tortillas
- [ ] 1 (16.3 oz.) tube "Grands" refrigerated biscuits
- [ ] 2 (12.4 oz.) tubes refrigerated cinnamon rolls with icing
- [ ] 1 round loaf ciabatta bread
- [ ] 8 oz. spaghetti
- [ ] 1 box granola cereal *(or the ingredients for homemade, p. 13)*

Eggs & Meat

- [ ] 1 lb. ground breakfast sausage
- [ ] 1 lb. Italian sausage
- [ ] 2 lbs. ground beef
- [ ] 5 to 6 oz. deli-sliced turkey
- [ ] 8 large slices Canadian bacon
- [ ] 9 eggs
- [ ] 1 (3 oz.) jar bacon bits

Canned Goods

- [ ] 1 (15 oz.) can tomato sauce
- [ ] 1 small can french fried onions
- [ ] 1 (8 oz.) can crushed pineapple
- [ ] 1 (21 oz.) can blueberry pie filling
- [ ] 1 (24 oz.) jar marinara sauce

Spices, Oils & Sauces

- [ ] 1 (1 oz.) pkg. taco seasoning
- [ ] Apple jelly
- [ ] Prepared basil pesto
- [ ] BBQ sauce *(or the ingredients for homemade, p.43)*
- [ ] Ranch dressing
- [ ] 1 C. salsa

Other

- [ ] 4 (1 oz.) bags corn chips
- [ ] 4 fruit or gelatin cups
- [ ] Mini M&Ms and marshmallows
- [ ] Milk chocolate chips

Plus staples listed on page 3

5

AVOCADO BREAKFAST BOATS
with Sweet Tortilla Roll-Ups

Spread 4 flour tortillas with softened butter and sprinkle generously with cinnamon-sugar. Roll up, spritz with cooking spray, and wrap in foil; set on a grate over medium coals until warm. Meanwhile, halve 2 avocados and remove pits. Scoop out a little of each center to make room for an egg; mash and reserve. Set each half upright in a nest of foil placed on a larger piece of foil. Crack 1 egg into each avocado half and sprinkle with 1 T. each bacon bits and shredded Monterey Jack cheese; season with salt and pepper. Seal outer foil around nests and set on coals for 15 minutes, rotating several times but keeping upright. Spoon reserved mashed avocado on top and serve with Sweet Tortilla Roll-Ups.

MAKE-AHEAD PICNIC LOAF

Slice 2 zucchini and ½ (16 oz.) pkg. baby bell peppers; **reserve ½ C. zucchini slices for Day 3 Dinner**. Toss remaining veggies with 2 T. olive oil and 1 tsp. garlic powder. Spread on a grill pan and cook on a grate over hot coals until tender and charred; let cool. Meanwhile, cut the top off a round loaf of ciabatta bread and set "lid" aside. Hollow out the middle of loaf, leaving a shell.* Spread 3 T. prepared pesto on inside of shell and lid. Using 5 to 6 oz. each sliced swiss cheese and deli-sliced turkey, fill bread shell with two alternating layers of cheese, grilled veggies, turkey, and spinach or lettuce;** season with salt and pepper as desired. Press lid down and wrap tightly in plastic wrap. Chill 2 hours or overnight. Slice into wedges and serve.

* Reserve removed bread to prep meatballs for Day 1 Dinner.

** Remaining greens will be used on Days 2 and 3.

MEATBALL STEW PACKS
with Garlic Biscuits

1 lb. each ground beef and Italian sausage

2 C. crumbled ciabatta bread*

⅓ C. milk

1 egg

3 T. grated Parmesan cheese

1 small head cabbage, sliced

1 large onion, sliced, divided

Garlic salt and black pepper to taste

1 (15 oz.) can tomato sauce

1 T. vegetable oil

Butter

1 (16.3 oz.) tube "Grands" refrigerated biscuits *(or fry a double batch of Homemade Biscuits, recipe on page 9)*

In a big bowl, combine meats, bread, milk, egg, and Parmesan cheese; mix well. Form into 28 (1½") meatballs. Divide all the cabbage and most of the onion among 4 (18") doubled squares of heavy-duty foil. Place four meatballs in each pack and season with garlic salt and pepper. Divide tomato sauce among the packs and seal foil well.

Place the remaining onion and all remaining meatballs in another big foil pack, sealing well.

Set all packs on medium-hot coals and cook 20 to 30 minutes or until meat is done, rotating packs several times. Meanwhile, heat oil and 1 T. butter in a 12" skillet. Add biscuits and sprinkle with garlic salt; cover with foil and fry slowly until puffed up, cooked through, and golden brown on both sides, turning once. **Reserve four biscuits for Day 2 Breakfast**; serve the remaining biscuits with stew packs. Let plain meatball pack cool and then **reserve for Day 3 Dinner**.

* Use reserved bread from Day 1 Lunch.

HOMEMADE BISCUITS

For 4 (3") biscuits, mix 1 C. flour, 1½ tsp. baking powder, ½ tsp. salt, 3 T. nonfat dry milk, and 2 T. sugar in a bowl. Drizzle with 2 T. canola oil and mix with your fingers. To prepare, add seasonings or shredded cheese if desired, and stir in enough water (¼ to ½ C.) to get either a soft dough to shape and bake (see Camp Dogs, page 26) or a thick drop batter to skillet-fry in butter and oil (see Breakfast Burgers, page 10).

Breakfast Burgers

Wrap 4 biscuits* in foil and reheat near the fire. Meanwhile, shape 1 lb. breakfast sausage into four patties and cook in a skillet over medium-hot heat; remove and keep warm. Crack 4 eggs into the same skillet and cook as desired. Smear apple jelly on split biscuits. Fill each sandwich with 1 sausage patty, 2 T. french fried onions, 1 slice Colby-Jack cheese, and 1 egg. Serve with apple wedges.

Use fried biscuits reserved from Day 1 Dinner, or drop and fry four fresh Homemade Biscuits in a skillet with 1 T. each oil and butter following the recipe on page 9.

Aloha Quesadillas

Set 1 flour tortilla in a greased pie iron and top with 2 slices Canadian bacon, 2 T. shredded Monterey Jack cheese, 1 T. bacon bits, 2 T. crushed pineapple *(drained)*, and some french fried onions; drizzle with BBQ sauce to taste. Set another tortilla on top and close the iron; trim off edges and cook over hot coals until toasted on both sides. Repeat to make three more.
(These may also be cooked in a skillet, pressing firmly before flipping.)

WALKING TACOS
with Dessert Cups

1 lb. ground beef

1 (1 oz.) pkg. taco seasoning

1 C. salsa, divided

4 (1 oz.) pkgs. corn chips

½ to ¾ C. shredded Monterey Jack cheese

¼ bag lettuce or spinach, chopped*

½ pt. grape tomatoes, halved*

Sour cream

4 fruit or gelatin cups

Brown ground beef in a skillet over medium heat; drain and stir in taco seasoning and half the salsa. Crunch up the chips and open the bags; divide meat among bags and top with some cheese, lettuce, tomatoes, more salsa, and sour cream. Serve with chilled fruit or gelatin cups.

Any remaining greens and tomatoes can be used for Day 3 Lunch.

BLUEBERRY CINNAMON ROLLS
with Granola Cereal

1 pt. blueberries

1 (21 oz.) can blueberry pie filling

Zest and juice of 1 lemon

2 (12.4 oz.) tubes refrigerated cinnamon rolls

Granola cereal *(purchased or make Fireside Granola, recipe on page 13)*

2 C. milk

In an oiled 12" Dutch oven, combine blueberries, pie filling, zest, and juice. Cook over medium heat until bubbly, stirring often. Separate the rolls and arrange over blueberry mixture. Cover the pot and set on a ring of 12 hot coals, spreading 10 or 12 more coals on the lid. Bake 15 to 25 minutes or until golden brown and cooked through. After 10 minutes, rotate the pot and lid, remove 4 or 5 bottom coals, and replenish top coals for even baking. Check frequently until done. *(If you prefer to use a standard oven, bake at 350° about 20 minutes.)*

Scoop rolls and some blueberry topping onto serving plates and serve with bowls of granola and milk. Leftover rolls? They'll taste really good later today!

FIRESIDE GRANOLA

Layer 2 (18") lengths of heavy-duty foil and grease well. Dump 1½ C. chopped pecans, 4 C. quick-cooking oats, and ½ C. brown sugar onto foil and sprinkle with ¼ tsp. each cinnamon and salt; mix well. Stir in ⅓ C. coconut oil and seal foil around granola, pressing pack flat. Set on a grate over hot coals for 10 to 15 minutes to brown, turning and shaking pack occasionally. Drizzle granola with ¼ C. honey and 1 T. maple syrup; stir and let cool.

— Sweet Idea —

Use Fireside Granola to make yummy S'mores Cups. Just toss some into serving cups and top with mini marshmallows, milk chocolate chips, and mini M&Ms. A perfect snack or dessert!

LOADED BAKED POTATOES
with Garden Salad

Pierce the skins of 4 large russet potatoes and wrap each in foil.
Set in hot coals for 45 to 60 minutes or until tender, turning several
times. Meanwhile, coarsely chop the remaining lettuce or spinach and
toss with any remaining halved tomatoes *(from Day 2 tacos)*. Keep
salad cool. In a skillet over medium heat, melt 2 T. butter; sauté 8 oz.
sliced mushrooms and 12 asparagus stalks until tender.

To serve, slice potatoes and fluff up the insides. Top as you like with
the sautéed veggies,* and any leftover shredded cheese, french fried
onions, bacon bits, and sour cream; season with salt and pepper. Toss
lettuce salad with ranch dressing and serve alongside the potatoes.

* Reserve any leftover sautéed vegetables for tonight's dinner.

SPAGHETTI & MEATBALLS
with Veggie Platter & S'mores Cups

In a big pot of boiling water, cook 8 oz. spaghetti according to package directions. Meanwhile, combine reserved cooked meatballs *(from Day 1 Dinner)* and 1 (24 oz.) jar marinara sauce in a saucepan over medium heat until hot, stirring often. If desired, stir in any reserved sautéed veggies from Day 3 Lunch. To serve, drain spaghetti and divide among plates. Top with hot meatball sauce and grated Parmesan cheese. Serve with remaining grape tomatoes, mini bell peppers, asparagus spears, and reserved zucchini slices with ranch dressing for dipping.

Make S'mores Cups for dessert *(recipe on page 13)*.

TRIP 2 Menu at a Glance

Day 1

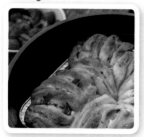

Bacon & Cheddar Pull-Aparts
Berry Bowl

Tex-Mex Rice
Melon Wedges

Glazed Frank Kabobs
Dinner Rolls

Day 2

Hot Mess on a Tortilla

Stuffed Portobellos
Garlic Toast

Grilled Chicken &
Brussels Sprouts

Day 3

Cheesy Southern Grits
Juice

Camp Dogs
Fresh Fruit

Chicken Taco Soup
Berry Angel Cakes

TRIP 2 Shopping List

Dairy

- [ ] 2 sticks butter
- [ ] 1 (7.5 oz.) tub chive & onion cream cheese spread
- [ ] 8 deli slices cheddar cheese
- [ ] 2 C. shredded mozzarella cheese
- [ ] 2 C. shredded Cheddar Jack cheese
- [ ] 1 C. shredded swiss cheese
- [ ] 1 (6 oz.) container vanilla yogurt
- [ ] Sour cream, optional

Fresh Fruits & Veggies

- [ ] 1 each green & red bell pepper
- [ ] 1 small red onion
- [ ] 1 pint cherry tomatoes
- [ ] 1 cantaloupe
- [ ] 1 bunch green onions
- [ ] 4 ears sweet corn
- [ ] 4 large Portobello mushrooms
- [ ] 12 oz. Brussels sprouts
- [ ] ½ lb. grapes
- [ ] 1 apple
- [ ] 1 pt. each blueberries, raspberries & strawberries

Breads & Grains

- [ ] 8 corn tortillas
- [ ] 1 C. long grain white rice
- [ ] 2 (16.3 oz.) cans "Grands" flaky layers refrigerated biscuits
- [ ] 1 loaf French bread
- [ ] 8 (1 oz.) packets instant grits
- [ ] 4 to 8 dinner rolls

Eggs & Meat

- [ ] 1 lb. spicy ground breakfast sausage
- [ ] 8 eggs
- [ ] 8 jumbo hot dogs *(2 oz. each)*
- [ ] 1 lb. bacon strips
- [ ] 6 boneless, skinless chicken breast halves

Canned Goods

- [ ] 1 (15 oz.) can black eye peas
- [ ] 2 (15 oz.) cans Mexican-style stewed tomatoes
- [ ] 1 (15 oz.) can black beans
- [ ] 1 (14.5 oz.) can diced tomatoes with roasted onion & garlic
- [ ] 1 (16 oz.) jar roasted red peppers
- [ ] 1 (11 oz.) can cheddar cheese soup

Spices, Oils & Sauces

- [ ] 1 (1 oz.) pkg. taco seasoning
- [ ] Granulated beef bouillon
- [ ] ½ C. chili sauce
- [ ] Spicy brown mustard
- [ ] Chicago Steak Seasoning, dry mustard, chili powder
- [ ] 1 C. Italian dressing
- [ ] Spices for Seasoning Mix, p.23

Other

- [ ] Your favorite fruit juice (4 C.)
- [ ] 4 angel food mini-cakes
- [ ] Spray whipped cream, optional

Plus staples listed on page 3

17

BACON & CHEDDAR PULL-APARTS
with Berry Bowl

2 (16.3 oz.) tubes "Grands" flaky layers refrigerated biscuits *(we used Honey Butter Flavor)*

⅔ C. chive & onion cream cheese spread

¾ lb. bacon, cooked & crumbled

4 green onions, finely chopped

8 deli slices cheddar cheese, quartered

1 C. each blueberries, raspberries, and chopped strawberries

1 (6 oz.) container vanilla yogurt

Grease a 9 x 9" aluminum baking pan and set inside a second one. Separate each biscuit into two layers. Spread about 1 tsp. cream cheese on each piece and top with 1 to 2 tsp. bacon, ½ tsp. green onion, and ¼ slice cheese. Make four stacks of eight layers. Set one stack on its side along the side of pan, starting in one corner *(side without filling should touch the edge of pan.)* Set a second stack in pan at right angles to first stack. Set remaining two stacks around edges to fill pan.

Set pan on risers in a large Dutch oven *(we used 3 canning jar rings)*. Cover with lid and place on a ring of 12 hot coals with a few more coals on lid. Bake 50 to 60 minutes or until puffy, browned, and no longer doughy. Rotate pot and lid every 15 minutes and check doneness several times, replenishing or removing coals as needed for even baking. *(If you prefer, bake the pan in a 350° oven about 1 hour or until done.)*

Combine berries and serve in bowls with yogurt on top.

BERRY ANGEL CAKES

To top off Day 3 Dinner (or any meal), use your extra raspberries and strawberries to make a quick dessert. Simply mash the berries together (about 1 C. each), with 1 T. sugar. Let stand a few minutes, until juicy. Divide berries among four angel food mini-cakes. If you're feeling fancy, top with some spray whipped cream. Delish!

TEX-MEX RICE
with Melon Wedges

Melt 2 T. butter in a big skillet; add 1 C. long grain white rice and sauté over medium-high heat 5 minutes until golden brown, stirring often. Mix 2 tsp. beef bouillon granules with 2 C. hot water and add to rice. Cover and cook 20 to 25 minutes or until tender. Drain and rinse 1 (15 oz.) can black eye peas; add to rice mixture along with 1 (14.5 oz.) can diced tomatoes with roasted garlic and onion. Stir in 2 sliced green onions, 1 tsp. minced garlic, and salt, pepper, and chili powder to taste. Cook until liquid is absorbed and everything is hot. Top with sour cream if you'd like. Slice ½ cantaloupe into four wedges to serve with the rice.

* Save any leftover Tex-Mex Rice for use in Taco Soup on Day 3.

GLAZED FRANK KABOBS
with Dinner Rolls

Slice 4 hot dogs and 2 ears of shucked sweet corn into 1" pieces; slice 1 red onion into wedges. Cut half each of a red and green bell pepper into 1" pieces *(store remaining peppers to use for Day 2 Breakfast)*. Alternately thread pieces of hot dog, corn, onion, bell pepper, and a few cherry tomatoes on skewers and set aside.

Combine ½ C. chili sauce, 3 T. brown sugar, and 2 T. spicy brown mustard in a bowl. Set kabobs and two full ears of shucked corn* on a grate over medium-low heat; brush skewers with some of the sauce mixture. Cover food with foil and grill about 5 minutes. Continue to cook slowly until veggies are tender, rotating corn and kabobs every 5 minutes and brushing skewers with more sauce. Serve with warm dinner rolls and butter.

* This extra grilled corn will be used in Taco Soup on Day 3.

HOT MESS ON A TORTILLA

1 lb. spicy ground breakfast sausage

½ each green and red bell pepper, diced

1 tsp. minced garlic

8 to 10 cherry tomatoes, diced

½ tsp. onion powder

1 to 2 tsp. All-Purpose Seasoning Mix *(recipe on page 23)*

4 corn tortillas

4 eggs

1 T. butter

Chive & onion cream cheese spread *(you'll have some left from Day 1)*

In a big pot, cook sausage until browned and crumbly; drain. Add bell peppers and garlic to the pot and cook until tender, stirring frequently. Stir in tomatoes, onion powder, and Seasoning Mix; cook 5 to 7 minutes more. Meanwhile wrap tortillas in foil and set near the fire until warm.

In another skillet, fry eggs in butter as desired. Smear a little cream cheese spread over the warm tortillas. Divide sausage mixture among tortillas and top each with an egg.

ALL-PURPOSE SEASONING MIX

Combine 2 T. each garlic powder and ground cumin, 1 T. each ground coriander, smoked paprika, and sea salt, and 1½ tsp. black pepper. Sprinkle on pieces of meat or stir into ground meat mixtures while cooking. To make a meat rub, mix 1½ T. seasoning mix with 3 to 4 T. olive oil and rub into chicken, beef, or pork before grilling. Store seasoning in a small airtight container.

Make-Ahead Tip

For RV cooking convenience, make the delicious All-Purpose Seasoning Mix ahead of time and store it with your supply of staples. It's incredibly versatile and infuses flavor into all kinds of dishes.

STUFFED PORTOBELLOS
with Garlic Toast

4 large Portobello mushrooms

1 C. Italian dressing

1 (16 oz.) jar roasted red peppers, chopped

2 C. shredded mozzarella cheese

½ loaf French bread

¼ C. softened butter

Garlic salt

Remove stems and gills from mushrooms and marinate with dressing in a zippered plastic bag for at least 1 hour. Drain and grill on stem side for 5 minutes. Flip over and fill caps with red peppers and cheese. Grill until cheese melts, 5 to 8 minutes more.

For the **garlic toast**, slice the bread into 1" pieces; spread one side with butter and sprinkle with garlic salt. Set on grill to toast both sides.

Campfire Fondue

Heat 1 (11 oz.) can of cheddar cheese soup and 1 C. shredded swiss cheese in a saucepan over warm coals, stirring until melted and smooth. Superb with leftover French bread!

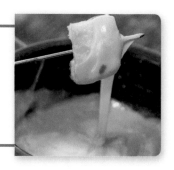

GRILLED CHICKEN
& Brussels Sprouts

12 oz. Brussels sprouts,
 par-cooked

2 T. spicy brown mustard

2 T. plus ¼ C. olive oil, divided

Salt and black pepper to taste

1½ T. All-Purpose Seasoning
 Mix *(recipe on page 23)*

6 boneless, skinless chicken
 breast halves*

½ loaf French bread

¼ C. softened butter

⅔ C. shredded Cheddar Jack cheese

Toss sprouts into a bowl with mustard, 2 T. oil, and salt and pepper to taste; let marinate about 30 minutes. Meanwhile, combine Seasoning Mix and remaining ¼ C. oil in a small bowl. Rub mixture over chicken pieces and set aside.

To cook, thread sprouts on skewers. Grill chicken breasts and sprouts skewers on an oiled grate over medium-hot coals for 3 to 6 minutes per side or until meat is done and sprouts are tender. Meanwhile, slice bread in half lengthwise; spread cut sides with butter and sprinkle with cheese. Toast on the grill until melty.

Let four chicken pieces rest a few minutes before serving with the sprouts. Allow the remaining two pieces of chicken to cool completely, then shred or chop the meat and chill; **reserve for use in Taco Soup on Day 3.**

* You'll grill all six chicken pieces, but only eat four at this meal.

Cheesy Southern Grits

Whisk 4 eggs with 2 T. water in a small bowl. Cook ¼ lb. bacon in a skillet until crisp; drain bacon strips and crumble, reserving grease in skillet. Cook the eggs in the bacon grease, stirring often, until fluffy and done. In each of four serving bowls, mix 2 (1 oz.) pkgs. instant grits with boiling water as directed on package. Stir in butter, salt, and pepper to taste. Top each serving of grits with some scrambled eggs, 2 to 3 T. shredded Cheddar Jack cheese,* and crumbled bacon. Serve with juice.

* Reserve remaining cheese for tonight's Taco Soup.

Camp Dogs & Fruit

Cube ½ cantaloupe and 1 apple; combine with 1 C. blueberries, and ½ lb. red or green grapes in a big bowl. Toss fruit together with a squeeze of honey and set aside. Mix ingredients for **Homemade Biscuits** as directed on page 9 to make a soft dough, adding ½ tsp. dry mustard and 1 tsp. Chicago Steak Seasoning. Wrap a walnut-sized piece of dough around 4 hot dogs, leaving ends exposed. Poke a camp fork or stick through each dog and dough and cook slowly over hot embers until crust is golden brown and dogs are hot. Serve with prepped fruit.

CHICKEN TACO SOUP
with Tortilla Crisps

2 (15 oz.) cans Mexican-style
  stewed tomatoes

2 ears grilled corn,
  cut from the cobs*

½ to 1 C. Tex-Mex Rice**

1 (15 oz.) can black beans

1 (1 oz.) pkg. taco
  seasoning mix

4 corn tortillas

Cooking spray

Salt

⅔ C. shredded Cheddar Jack
  cheese

In a big pot, combine tomatoes,
corn, rice, beans, and taco
seasoning. Stir well and set
over heat until hot and bubbly.
Meanwhile, spritz tortillas with
cooking spray and cut into
wedges; sprinkle with salt. Set
wedges on a big piece of foil on
the grate and cook until browned
on both sides. Top soup with
cheese and tortilla wedges.

For dessert, make Berry Angel
Cakes (recipe on page 19).

Reserved from Day 1 Dinner

**Leftovers from Day 1 Lunch*

TRIP 3 *Menu at a Glance*

Day 1

Breakfast Pitas
Melon Wedges

Stuffed Mexi-Burgers

Thai Chicken Kabobs
Grilled Cauliflower

Day 2

Strawberry Frenchies
Bacon

Chicken & Apple Salad
Cinnamon Muffins

Cajun Shrimp Pot

Day 3

Sausage-Filled Pancakes
Fruit Combo

Southwest Chicken Bake
Melon Wedges

Steak & Taters

TRIP 3 Shopping List

Dairy

- ☐ 2 sticks butter
- ☐ 2 C. shredded Mexican cheese
- ☐ 8 slices American cheese
- ☐ ½ C. crumbled blue cheese
- ☐ 1¼ C. milk

Fresh Fruits & Veggies

- ☐ 1 red bell pepper
- ☐ 2 green bell peppers
- ☐ 3 small onions
- ☐ 1 large tomato
- ☐ 1 melon of choice
- ☐ 1 bunch green onions
- ☐ 8 oz. sliced mushrooms
- ☐ 1 head cauliflower
- ☐ 2 red apples
- ☐ 1 pt. strawberries
- ☐ 1 head Romaine lettuce
- ☐ 9 or 10 small golden potatoes

Breads & Grains

- ☐ 8 (8") flour tortillas
- ☐ 4 whole pita pockets
- ☐ 1 C. long grain white rice
- ☐ 1 loaf white bread
- ☐ 4 hamburger buns
- ☐ 1½ C. biscuit baking mix or Make-Ahead Pancake Mix *(recipe on page 37)*

Eggs & Meat

- ☐ 1½ lbs. ground beef
- ☐ 12 eggs
- ☐ ¾ lb. bacon strips
- ☐ 6 boneless, skinless chicken breast halves
- ☐ 1 C. walnut halves
- ☐ 8 sausage patties (12 oz.)
- ☐ 1¼ to 2 lbs. flank steak
- ☐ 12 oz. frozen fully cooked shrimp

Canned Goods

- ☐ 1 (4 oz.) can diced green chiles
- ☐ 1 (10.75 oz.) can cream of celery soup
- ☐ 2 (10.75 oz.) cans cream of mushroom soup
- ☐ 2 (10 oz.) cans diced tomatoes with green chiles
- ☐ 1 C. unsweetened applesauce
- ☐ Strawberry preserves

Spices, Oils & Sauces

- ☐ Salsa
- ☐ 1 (1 oz.) packet dry onion soup mix
- ☐ Mayo, Thai sweet chili sauce, hot sauce, Sriracha sauce & soy sauce
- ☐ Pure maple syrup
- ☐ Balsamic salad dressing
- ☐ Cajun seasoning, cayenne pepper, red pepper flakes, ground ginger, nutmeg
- ☐ Apple cider vinegar

Plus staples listed on page 3

BREAKFAST PITAS
with Melon Wedges

Wrap 4 whole pita pockets *(halved)* in foil and set near the fire to warm. In a big skillet over medium heat, heat 2 T. vegetable oil; add 1 small onion *(chopped)*, 1 green bell pepper *(chopped)*, and 5 small golden potatoes *(diced)*; season with seasoned salt and black pepper. Cook until tender, stirring occasionally. Meanwhile, in a bowl, whisk 7 eggs with 3 T. water and a little salt. Heat 2 T. oil in another skillet; add eggs and scramble until cooked but still shiny. Fill each warm pita half with a slice of American cheese, some eggs, and some potato mixture. Serve with hot sauce and thin melon wedges, if you'd like.

STUFFED MEXI-BURGERS

Shape 1½ lbs. ground beef into eight thin patties. Drain 1 (4 oz.) can diced green chiles; divide the chiles among four of the patties. Top each with 2 T. shredded Mexican cheese, a sprinkle of cayenne pepper, and salt to taste. Top with remaining patties and press edges together well to seal fillings inside. Grill on greased foil set on a grate over medium coals until done, flipping once. Serve on toasted buns topped with lettuce leaves, sliced tomato, and salsa. Add a side of chips if you'd like. **Reserve the remaining lettuce for Day 2 Lunch.**

THAI CHICKEN KABOBS
with Grilled Cauliflower

6 boneless, skinless chicken breast halves, divided

Olive oil

Salt and black pepper to taste

1 red bell pepper

1 onion

1 head cauliflower

½ to 1 tsp. red pepper flakes

½ to 1 tsp. garlic powder

¼ C. each mayonnaise and Thai sweet chili sauce

Sriracha hot sauce

Leave three chicken pieces whole and brush with oil; season with salt and pepper and set aside. Cut the bell pepper, onion, and remaining three chicken pieces into 1" chunks. Alternately thread the chunks of chicken, bell pepper, and onion onto skewers and set aside. Cut the cauliflower into large florets. Brush the skewers and cauliflower with oil and sprinkle with salt and pepper. Stir together pepper flakes and garlic powder; sprinkle mixture over cauliflower only.

Arrange cauliflower on a grill pan, cover with foil, and cook over medium heat until roasted and tender, 8 to 10 minutes per side. Set skewers and the three whole chicken pieces on the oiled grate and cook over medium heat until done, rotating and turning as needed *(whole pieces will take longer to cook)*. Meanwhile, mix mayo, chili sauce, and a few drops of hot sauce. Serve skewers and dipping sauce alongside the cauliflower. Allow whole chicken pieces to cool, then chop and pack in an airtight container and **reserve for Lunches on Days 2 and 3**.

CINNAMON MUFFINS

Preheat the oven to 375° and line a muffin pan with 12 liners. In a bowl, whisk together 2 C. flour, ¾ C. sugar, 2 tsp. baking powder, 1 tsp. cinnamon, a dash of nutmeg, and ¼ tsp. salt. Add 1 beaten egg, 1 C. unsweetened applesauce, and ½ C. melted butter, stirring until just blended. Scoop into liners and sprinkle with sugar. Bake 18 to 20 minutes. Let cool. Pack in an airtight container to take on your trip.

Strawberry Frenchies
& BACON

Cook ¾ lb. bacon strips in a skillet over medium heat until crisp; drain. Meanwhile, whisk together 3 eggs, ¼ C. milk, and 1 tsp. cinnamon-sugar. Dip one side of a bread slice into egg mixture and set in a greased pie iron, egg side down. Spread with strawberry preserves; arrange ¼ C. sliced strawberries over preserves. Dip another bread slice in egg and place it on top, egg side up. Close iron and cook in hot embers until toasted on both sides. Repeat to make three more. Serve with maple syrup and a few bacon strips per person; crumble the remaining **cooked bacon and reserve for today's lunch**.

Chicken & Apple Salad
& CINNAMON MUFFINS

In a bowl, whisk together ⅓ C. balsamic salad dressing, 1 T. honey, and ¼ tsp. garlic powder. Core 2 apples and slice into wedges; toss with dressing mixture. Remove apples and set dressing aside; grill apples on an oiled grill pan over medium heat until crisp-tender and lightly browned. Tear up reserved lettuce *(from Day 1 Lunch)* and toss with set-aside dressing, 1 C. walnut halves, and ½ C. crumbled blue cheese; divide among serving bowls. Divide 1 C. of the reserved chopped grilled chicken *(from Day 1 Dinner)*, the reserved crumbled bacon *(from Breakfast)*, and the grilled apples among bowls and serve with Cinnamon Muffins *(recipe on page 33)*.

CAJUN SHRIMP POT

Butter

1 onion, diced

8 oz. sliced mushrooms

1 green bell pepper, diced

1 C. long grain white rice

2 tsp. Cajun seasoning

1 (10.75 oz.) can cream of mushroom soup

1 (10 oz.) can diced tomatoes with green chilies

2 C. water

Bread

Paprika

1 (12 oz.) pkg. frozen fully cooked shrimp *(deveined, tails on, thawed)*

In a 10" Dutch oven over medium heat, melt ¼ C. butter; sauté onion for 5 minutes. Stir in the next seven ingredients. Bring to a boil, then cover and simmer on a ring of hot coals with a few more on the lid. Cook until rice is tender, 15 to 20 minutes, rotating pot and lid twice and stirring once. Butter any leftover bread from breakfast, sprinkle with paprika, and toast both sides on a grate. Add shrimp to the pot, cover, and cook just until heated through. Serve in bowls with toast.

SAUSAGE-FILLED PANCAKES
with Fruit Combo

1 T. butter

½ C. pure maple syrup

¾ to 1 C. milk, divided

8 sausage patties

1½ C. biscuit baking mix *(or Make-Ahead Pancake Mix, recipe on page 37)*

2 T. sugar

¼ tsp. cinnamon

1 egg

½ tsp. vanilla

Sliced strawberries and ¼ melon, cut into chunks*

Put butter in a small metal bowl near the fire. When melted, whisk in syrup and 2 T. milk and keep sauce warm.

Meanwhile, cook sausage patties on a griddle or big skillet over medium heat until done, turning once; drain on paper towels. Wipe off griddle and let cool.

In a medium bowl, stir together baking or pancake mix with sugar and cinnamon. Whisk in egg, vanilla, and ⅔ C. milk plus a little more as needed to get a smooth pancake batter *(pourable but thick enough to hold a 3" to 4" shape on the griddle)*. Set aside.

Oil the griddle and set over medium-low heat. For each pancake, pour a large spoonful of batter on griddle *(slightly bigger than a sausage patty)* and set a cooked patty in the middle; cover with more batter and cook slowly until golden brown on both sides and no longer doughy. Serve with warm syrup sauce and fruit.

* *Use reserved berries and melon from previous days' breakfasts. Save some melon for Day 3 Lunch.*

MAKE-AHEAD PANCAKE MIX

In a bowl, whisk together 1⅓ C. flour, 2 tsp. baking powder, and ¼ tsp. salt. Add 1½ T. vegetable oil and mix it in with your hands. Make it before your trip and store in an airtight container at room temperature for several weeks. Use this mixture in place of 1½ C. biscuit baking mix to make Sausage-Filled Pancakes on page 36.

SOUTHWEST CHICKEN BAKE
with Melon Wedges

2 C. chopped chicken*

1½ C. shredded Mexican cheese, divided

1 (10.75 oz.) can cream of mushroom soup

1 (10.75 oz.) can cream of celery soup

1 (10 oz.) can diced tomatoes with green chilies

¾ C. sliced green onions

8 flour tortillas, cut into small pieces

4 melon wedges**

In the oiled pot of a 10" Dutch oven, combine chicken, 1 C. cheese, both soups, tomatoes, and onions. Stir in tortilla pieces. Cover pot with lid and set on a ring of 11 hot coals; arrange 11 more coals on the lid. Cook 20 to 30 minutes or until hot and bubbly, rotating pot and lid several times. Remove lid, sprinkle with remaining ½ C. cheese and let melt. Serve with melon wedges.

* Use reserved grilled and chopped chicken from Day 1 Dinner.

** Use melon that remains after Breakfast on Days 1 and 3.

STEAK & TATERS

¼ C. plus ⅓ C. vegetable oil, divided

3 T. soy sauce

1½ T. each apple cider vinegar and honey

½ tsp. each garlic powder and ground ginger

1¼ to 2 lbs. flank steak

1 (1 oz.) pkg. dry onion soup mix

4 to 5 golden potatoes, scrubbed

In a large zippered plastic bag, combine ¼ C. oil, soy sauce, vinegar, honey, garlic powder, and ginger; mix well. Add steak to bag, seal, and turn to coat meat; chill for 24 hours, turning occasionally. In another bag, combine soup mix and remaining ⅓ C. oil. Cut potatoes into bite-size pieces and add to the bag; mix well and let marinate 30 to 60 minutes.

When ready to cook, fry the potatoes in an oiled skillet on a grate over medium heat for 30 minutes or until tender, stirring occasionally. Grill the steak on oiled grate to desired doneness. Thinly slice meat across the grain and serve with potatoes *(and any leftover muffins from Day 2 Lunch).*

Day 1

Deep Dish Breakfast Pizza
Apple Juice

Brats & 'Kraut

Grilled Salmon Dinner

Day 2

Rise & Shine Kabobs

Dutch Oven Lasagna
Breadsticks

Pork Chops with Cheesy Fries
Creamy Coleslaw

Day 3

Pie Iron Omelet

BBQ Ham Sliders
Celery Sticks

Grandma's Hot Dish

TRIP 4 Shopping List

Dairy

- [ ] 1 (12 oz.) bottle squeeze butter
- [ ] 2 C. shredded cheddar cheese
- [ ] 4 C. shredded mozzarella cheese
- [ ] 1 can grated Parmesan cheese
- [ ] 1 (12 oz.) tub cottage cheese

Fresh Fruits & Veggies

- [ ] 3 small onions *(2 red, 1 yellow)*
- [ ] 1 pineapple
- [ ] 4 bell peppers *(3 green, 1 other)*
- [ ] 1 bunch green onions
- [ ] 7 or 8 small red potatoes
- [ ] 2 nectarines
- [ ] 1 (16 oz.) pkg. shredded cabbage with carrots
- [ ] 1 bunch celery

Breads & Grains

- [ ] 21 wonton wrappers
- [ ] 1 (8 oz.) tube refrigerated crescent dough sheet
- [ ] 1 lb. frozen pizza dough
- [ ] 4 to 6 brat buns
- [ ] 12 slider buns
- [ ] Purchased breadsticks

Eggs & Meat

- [ ] 10 eggs
- [ ] ¾ lb. bacon strips
- [ ] 12 sausage links *(with skins)*
- [ ] 1 lb. deli-sliced ham
- [ ] ½ lb. ground beef
- [ ] 1 lb. ground Italian sausage
- [ ] 1½ lbs. ground turkey
- [ ] 4 to 6 bratwurst
- [ ] 4 (6 oz.) bone-in pork chops
- [ ] 4 (4 oz.) salmon fillets *(fresh or frozen)*

Canned Goods

- [ ] 1 (10.75 oz.) can cream of chicken soup
- [ ] ¼ C. unsweetened applesauce
- [ ] 1 (15 oz.) can sauerkraut
- [ ] 1 (24 oz.) jar marinara sauce
- [ ] 1 (15 oz.) can mixed vegetables

Spices, Oils & Sauces

- [ ] Soy & Worcestershire sauce, apple cider vinegar
- [ ] ¾ C. mayonnaise
- [ ] 1 C. ketchup
- [ ] Dijon & whole grain mustard
- [ ] Dried parsley, caraway seed
- [ ] Ground oregano & thyme
- [ ] Apple jelly

Other

- [ ] 4 (8 oz.) bottles apple juice
- [ ] 14 to 16 oz. frozen french fries
- [ ] 8 to 12 oz. beer
- [ ] 2 (9 x 9") foil pans

Plus staples listed on page 3

DEEP DISH BREAKFAST PIZZA
with Apple Juice

¾ lb. bacon strips

½ red onion, diced

½ lb. ground Italian sausage

1 lb. frozen pizza dough, thawed

1 C. each shredded cheddar and mozzarella cheese

4 eggs

2 T. water

Garlic powder, salt, and black pepper to taste

Grated Parmesan cheese

Apple juice*

Cook bacon in the pot of a 10" Dutch oven over medium-high heat until crisp; drain on paper towels and pour off grease. Crumble bacon and **reserve ⅓ C. for Day 2 Dinner**; put remainder into a big bowl. Cook onion and sausage in the pot until meat is browned and crumbly. Remove from heat and add meat mixture to bowl with bacon; set aside. Let the pot cool, then wipe out excess grease. Line pot with foil and grease lightly. Press dough over the bottom of pot and 1" up the side. Cover with lid and set on a ring of 7 hot coals. Partially bake crust for 5 to 8 minutes.

Press meat mixture into partially baked crust; sprinkle with shredded cheeses. In a bowl, whisk together eggs, water, and seasonings; pour evenly over ingredients in crust, letting it seep in without overflowing. Sprinkle with Parmesan cheese. Cover and set on a ring of 7 hot coals with 12 more coals scattered on lid. Bake 20 to 25 minutes or until crust is golden brown and eggs are puffed and set. Rotate pot and lid several times and move coals as needed for even baking. Let stand 5 minutes, then lift foil to remove pizza. Slice and serve with juice.

* Reserve ¼ C. apple juice for Homemade BBQ Sauce (recipe in sidebar on this page).

BBQ SAUCE

In a small saucepan over medium-low heat, combine 1 C. ketchup, ¼ C. each unsweetened applesauce and apple juice, 2½ T. apple cider vinegar, 2 T. Worcestershire sauce, 1 tsp. Dijon mustard, ¼ tsp. each garlic powder and onion powder, ½ tsp. salt, and ⅛ tsp. black pepper. Simmer about 15 minutes, until slightly thickened. Cool completely and transfer to an airtight container. Use on ham sandwiches, or with pork chops, brats, or pie iron omelets.

BRATS & 'KRAUT

4 to 6 bratwurst

1 (15 oz.) can sauerkraut, drained

½ C. sugar

½ tsp. caraway seed

3 T. squeeze butter spread

8 to 12 oz. beer

4 to 6 brat buns

Condiments: mustard, BBQ sauce *(recipe on page 43)* diced green bell pepper* and red onion*

Place bratwurst in a 9 x 9" foil pan and set the pan inside a second one. Spread sauerkraut over brats and sprinkle evenly with sugar and caraway seed. Drizzle the squeeze butter spread over the top and slowly pour beer over everything *(without overflowing pan)*. Cover tightly with foil and set on a level grate over medium-high heat to cook for 30 to 45 minutes or until brats are done. Serve brats and sauerkraut on buns with condiments of choice.

* Dice ½ green bell pepper and ½ red onion; reserve remainders for later needs.

GRILLED SALMON DINNER

1 fresh pineapple, peeled,
  halved lengthwise & cored

½ red onion

1 green bell pepper, cored

Vegetable oil

4 (4 oz.) salmon fillets
  (thawed if frozen)

½ tsp. each salt, ground
  oregano, ground thyme,
  and garlic powder

1 tsp. black pepper

Apple jelly

Creamy Coleslaw, optional
  (recipe on page 49)

Cut half the pineapple into 1" chunks and **reserve for Day 2 Breakfast**. Cut the remaining pineapple half and onion into wedges and cut bell pepper into 2" pieces. Set pineapple wedges and vegetables on an oiled grill pan and brush all sides of food with oil. Brush both sides of salmon with oil and place in an oiled grill basket. In a small bowl, mix all seasonings and sprinkle over both sides of the salmon, onion, and bell pepper pieces; brush pineapple wedges with apple jelly. Let food rest at least 20 minutes *(up to 1 hour)*. Cook on a grate over medium-low heat for 6 to 10 minutes per side or until salmon flakes easily and everything is hot and lightly browned. Serve with coleslaw if you'd like.

RISE & SHINE KABOBS

Pit 2 nectarines and slice into wedges. Cut 3 red potatoes into thin wedges and cut half each of a green and orange *(or red)* bell pepper into 1" pieces.* Slice 12 breakfast sausage links in half. Using the reserved pineapple chunks from Day 1 Dinner, alternately thread pieces of pineapple, nectarine, potato, bell peppers, and sausage onto four skewers. Cook skewers on an oiled grate over medium-low heat about 15 minutes, turning often and brushing with apple jelly, until sausage is done, potatoes are tender, and fruit is lightly browned.

* Reserve and dice the remaining bell pepper halves for Day 3 Breakfast.

DUTCH OVEN LASAGNA

In the pot of a 10" Dutch oven, cook ½ lb. each ground beef and Italian sausage over medium heat until browned and crumbly. Remove from heat, drain, and spoon meat into a big bowl; cool slightly. Stir in 1 (12 oz.) tub cottage cheese, ½ C. grated Parmesan cheese, 1 egg, 1 T. dried parsley, and ½ tsp. onion powder. Spread ¼ (24 oz.) jar marinara sauce *(generous ½ C.)* over bottom of pot. Layer 7 wonton wrappers over sauce. Spread half the meat mixture over wrappers and cover with ½ C. sauce and ¾ C. shredded mozzarella cheese. Repeat with another layer of wrappers, meat, sauce, and mozzarella. Top with seven more wrappers and all remaining sauce. Cover pot and set on a ring of 11 hot coals with 11 more coals on lid. Cook 20 to 30 minutes or until hot and bubbly, rotating pot and lid twice and moving coals as needed for even cooking. Remove lid and sprinkle with ¾ C. mozzarella *(save any leftover cheese for Day 3 lunch)*. Cover, add coals to lid, and cook 10 minutes more to melt cheese. Let rest 15 minutes. Serve with breadsticks.

GRILLED PORK CHOPS
with Cheesy Fries & Coleslaw

¼ C. honey

2 T. each Dijon and whole grain mustard and apple cider vinegar

1 T. soy sauce

1 tsp. minced garlic

Salt and black pepper to taste

4 (6 oz.) pork chops

14 to 16 oz. frozen french fries *(partially thawed)*

2 T. squeeze butter spread

½ C. shredded cheddar cheese

½ C. sliced green onions

⅓ C. cooked, crumbled bacon*

Creamy Coleslaw *(recipe on page 49)*

In big zippered plastic bag, combine honey, both mustards, vinegar, soy sauce, garlic, salt, and pepper. Knead the bag until well mixed. Add chops, zip bag closed, and turn several times to coat in sauce. Marinate at least 30 minutes *(or overnight in the fridge)*.

When ready to cook, divide fries among 2 (15") pieces of foil. Drizzle with butter spread, toss well, and spread in a single layer. Fold foil edges around fries to form a nest that's open at the top. Set packs on a grate over indirect heat, cover loosely with another piece of foil, and cook 30 to 40 minutes or until browned and hot, turning fries once or twice. Divide cheese, onions, and bacon evenly among fries and set over fire until melted.

Meanwhile, remove chops from bag and grill on an oiled grate over medium-high heat until browned on both sides and thoroughly cooked, 3 to 5 minutes per side *(internal temperature of 145°)*. Let chops rest a few minutes before serving with the fries and Creamy Coleslaw.

* Use reserved bacon from Day 1 Breakfast.

CREAMY COLESLAW

Combine ½ (16 oz.) pkg. classic shredded cabbage (4 to 5 C.),* ½ C. chopped red onion, ½ C. diced green pepper, and 2 celery ribs (chopped) in a bowl. In another bowl, whisk together ¾ C. mayonnaise, 2 T. each sugar, apple cider vinegar, and olive oil, 1 tsp. sea salt, and black pepper to taste. Add to salad mixture and toss well. Chill until needed.

* Reserve all remaining shredded cabbage for Day 3 Lunch and Dinner.

Pie Iron Omelet

Dice enough sliced ham to measure 1 C. and toss into a bowl.* Add ½ C. each diced bell peppers *(reserve remainder for tonight's Dinner)* and diced yellow onion *(reserved from Day 2 Breakfast)*. In another bowl, scramble 5 eggs with 2 T. water; cook in a buttered skillet over medium heat until fluffy. Unroll 1 (8 oz.) tube refrigerated crescent dough sheet and cut into eight equal pieces. Press one piece into a greased pie iron and add ¼ each of the eggs and ham mixture and 2 T. shredded cheddar cheese. Cover with another dough piece and close pie iron. Cook in hot coals until golden brown on both sides. Repeat to make three more.

* Reserve remaining sliced ham for Day 3 Lunch.

BBQ Ham Sliders
& CELERY STICKS

Layer reserved sliced ham *(from Day 3 Breakfast)* on a large doubled piece of foil and wrap well; set on a grate over medium heat until heated through, about 15 minutes. Butter the cut sides of 8 slider buns and toast on a grate until lightly browned. Sprinkle 2 or 3 T. shredded mozzarella cheese on each bun bottom and top with warm ham, some of the remaining shredded cabbage, BBQ Sauce *(recipe on page 43)*, and bun top. Serve with celery sticks.

GRANDMA'S HOT DISH

2 T. vegetable oil

1½ lbs. ground turkey

½ to ¾ C. diced yellow onion *(use what remains after today's breakfast)*

1 tsp. garlic powder

Salt and black pepper to taste

1 (15 oz.) can mixed vegetables

Leftover shredded cabbage *(about 1 C.)*

4 or 5 red potatoes, sliced

1 (10.75 oz.) can cream of chicken soup

4 slider buns, buttered

Heat oil in a 10" Dutch oven over medium-high heat. Add turkey, onion, and seasonings, and cook until meat is browned and crumbly. Stir in mixed vegetables and cabbage, then layer the potatoes over meat mixture. Spread soup over the potatoes. Cover and cook on a ring of 5 hot coals with 10 to 12 more coals on the lid for 25 to 30 minutes or until potatoes are tender and everything is hot and bubbly. Rotate pot and lid several times during cooking. Toast the slider buns and serve with the casserole.

TRIP 5 *Menu at a Glance*

Day 1

Oatmeal Supreme

Pepperoni Pasta Salad

Dutch Oven Pot Roast

Day 2

Stuffed French Toast

BBQ Beef Sandwiches
Carrot Sticks

Lemonade Chicken
Pecan Sweet Potatoes

Day 3

Skillet Breakfast Hash

Chicken Noodle Soup
& Grilled Cheese

Flatbread Pizzas
Grilled Green Beans

Dairy

- [ ] 2 sticks butter
- [ ] 2 C. milk
- [ ] 2 (6 oz.) cartons vanilla yogurt
- [ ] 3 (8 oz.) blocks of cheese *(1 mozzarella, 2 cheddar)*
- [ ] 1 C. shredded Parmesan cheese
- [ ] 2 (8 oz.) pkgs. cream cheese

Fresh Fruits & Veggies

- [ ] 2 bell peppers *(any color)*
- [ ] 1 bunch celery
- [ ] 1 bunch green onions
- [ ] 2 medium yellow onions
- [ ] ¾ to 1 lb. green beans
- [ ] 8 oz. sliced mushrooms
- [ ] 4 medium tomatoes
- [ ] 2 lbs. medium carrots
- [ ] 3 lbs. golden potatoes
- [ ] 4 sweet potatoes
- [ ] 5 fresh peaches *(or 16 oz. frozen)*
- [ ] 1 lemon

Breads & Grains

- [ ] 2⅔ C. old-fashioned oats
- [ ] 6 oz. small shell pasta
- [ ] 1½ C. egg noodles
- [ ] 1 loaf bread *(cinnamon-swirl or white)*
- [ ] 6 to 8 hamburger buns
- [ ] 4 flatbread pizza crusts

Eggs & Meat

- [ ] ¾ C. chopped pecans
- [ ] 1 (5 to 6 oz.) pkg. pepperoni
- [ ] 1 (4 to 5 lb.) beef chuck roast
- [ ] 1 (4½ lb.) whole chicken
- [ ] ¾ to 1 C. bacon bits
- [ ] 6 eggs

Canned Goods

- [ ] 1 (4 oz.) can sliced black olives
- [ ] 2 (14.5 oz.) cans beef broth
- [ ] 2 (14.5 oz.) cans chicken broth

Spices, Oils & Sauces

- [ ] Pure maple syrup
- [ ] 1⅓ C. BBQ sauce *(or ingredients for homemade, pg. 43)*
- [ ] 1 (16 oz.) bottle each Italian & ranch dressing
- [ ] 2 bay leaves
- [ ] Lemon pepper
- [ ] Dried basil & oregano
- [ ] ½ to 1 C. pizza sauce

Other

- [ ] ¼ C. each dried cranberries and chopped dates
- [ ] 1 (12 oz.) bag frozen red tart cherries
- [ ] 1 (12 oz.) can lemon-lime soda
- [ ] Snack crackers, optional

Plus staples listed on page 3

OATMEAL SUPREME

In a saucepan over medium heat, combine 1¾ C. each water and milk and bring to a boil. Stir in 2 C. old-fashioned oats, 1 tsp. cinnamon, and a dash of salt. Cook over low heat until it starts to thicken, 3 to 4 minutes, stirring occasionally. Stir in 2 T. maple syrup and ¼ C. each chopped dates, chopped pecans, and dried cranberries. Cook until heated through; cover and let stand for 5 minutes. Serve in bowls topped with vanilla yogurt.

PEPPERONI PASTA SALAD

Cook 6 oz. small **shell pasta** in boiling water as directed on package. Drain, rinse, and cool completely. Place pasta in a big bowl and add 1 C. chopped **pepperoni**, 1 (4 oz.) can sliced **black olives** *(drained)*, 4 oz. cubed **mozzarella cheese**, ½ C. shredded Parmesan cheese, 1 C. diced **bell pepper** *(any color)*, ½ C. diced **celery**, and ⅓ C. sliced **green onions**. Drizzle with about 1¼ C. **Italian dressing**. Gently fold in 1 diced **tomato**. Chill at least 20 minutes before serving.

Make-Ahead Tip

Cook, drain, and cool the pasta; stir in green onions, celery, and ¼ cup of the dressing, then cover and chill overnight. Stir in all remaining ingredients before serving.

DUTCH OVEN POT ROAST

1 (4 to 5) lb. beef chuck roast

Salt and black pepper to taste

2 to 3 T. olive oil

2 (14.5 oz.) cans beef broth

1 T. minced garlic

2 bay leaves

10 medium carrots

3 lbs. medium golden potatoes

2 celery ribs

1 C. chopped onion

Season roast generously with salt and pepper. Heat oil in the pot of a deep 12" Dutch oven over medium-high heat. Brown the roast on all sides, then reduce heat to medium-low. Add broth, garlic, and bay leaves; cover and simmer slowly for 1½ to 2 hours, with a few hot coals on the bottom and a few more on the lid *(or cook in a 350° oven)*.

Meanwhile, peel the carrots and slice into 1" pieces; cut potatoes and celery into 2" chunks. Add to the pot along with the onion. Cover and cook slowly about 1 hour longer or until everything is tender, using 6 to 8 hot coals under the pot and 8 more on the lid. Discard bay leaves. Let meat stand a few minutes before slicing. Serve about ⅔ each of the sliced roast, potatoes, and carrots with some of the cooking liquid; **reserve the remaining roast, potatoes, and carrots for later meals.***

* Chop the reserved beef; set aside 2½ to 3 C. for Day 2 Lunch and about ½ C. for Day 3 Breakfast. Reserve 3 to 4 cooked potatoes and 2 or 3 cooked carrots for Day 3 Breakfast.

PEACH & CHERRY CRISP

Thaw and combine 1 (12 oz.) bag frozen red tart cherries and 4 sliced fresh peaches (or ¾ (16 oz.) bag frozen peaches) in a doubled 9 x 9" foil pan. Stir in ¼ C. sugar and 2 T. water. In a bowl, mix ⅔ C. each old-fashioned oats and flour, ½ C. brown sugar, ⅓ C. melted butter, and ½ tsp. cinnamon; spread over fruit. Cover with greased foil and cook on a grate over medium heat 45 to 60 minutes. Move to warm embers and set coals on top of foil a few minutes to brown. Top with vanilla yogurt.

57

Stuffed French Toast

Dice 1 fresh **peach** *(or 1 C. frozen, thawed peaches)*. Mix ½ C. softened **cream cheese**, 2 T. **brown sugar**, and 1 tsp. **cinnamon**. Spread an equal amount of mixture on eight slices of **bread**. Arrange peaches on four of the slices and top with remaining bread. In a shallow bowl, mix 2 **eggs**, 2 T. **milk**, and 1 tsp. **vanilla**. Dip each side of a sandwich into egg mixture and set in a greased pie iron. Cook on hot coals until brown on both sides. Serve with **maple syrup**.

BBQ Beef Sandwiches
& CARROT STICKS

Slice 2 or 3 raw **carrots** into sticks and chill. Pour 1 C. **BBQ sauce** into a medium saucepan *(use your favorite bottled BBQ sauce or make the homemade sauce on page 43)*. Stir in 2½ to 3 C. chopped **roast beef** *(reserved from Day 1 Dinner)* and simmer over medium-low heat until sauce is reduced, stirring often. Spoon onto 4 **hamburger buns** and serve with carrot sticks.

LEMONADE CHICKEN
& Pecan Sweet Potatoes

1 (4½ lb.) whole chicken

Lemon pepper

1 (12 oz.) can lemon-lime soda

Juice of 1 lemon

4 sweet potatoes

¼ C. butter, melted

½ C. each brown sugar and chopped pecans

Rinse chicken and pat dry. Season inside and out with lemon-pepper. Pour soda and lemon juice into the pot of a deep 12" Dutch oven; set chicken inside *(breast side up)* and cover with lid. Cook about 1½ hours on a ring of 8 hot coals (with more coals on lid for browning), until meat tests done *(minimum 165°)*. Meanwhile, poke potatoes and wrap in foil. Bake in hot coals 45 to 60 minutes or until tender, turning twice. Mix butter, brown sugar, and pecans; cut potatoes open and top with pecan mixture. Slice or shred the chicken* and serve with potatoes. Cool the cooking liquid.*

* Reserve 1 C. cooked chicken and all cooking liquid for Day 3 Lunch. Any remaining chicken can be used for pizza on Day 3.

SKILLET BREAKFAST HASH

Cooked carrots and potatoes*

Vegetable oil

2 T. butter

½ C. diced onion

1 C. sliced mushrooms

1 C. sliced fresh green beans
 (1" pieces)**

1 tsp. minced garlic

½ C. chopped roast beef*

Salt and black pepper to taste

4 eggs

½ C. shredded cheddar
 cheese

1 tomato, diced

2 to 3 T. bacon bits,
 optional

Dice the cooked carrots and potatoes; set aside. Heat 2 T. oil and butter in a large skillet over medium heat. When hot and shimmery, add onion, mushrooms, and green beans; sauté about 5 minutes, until almost tender. Stir in garlic. Add diced carrots and potatoes to skillet and cook until lightly browned, flipping several times. Add roast beef. Season with salt and pepper and cook over medium-low heat until everything is hot. Push the hash to the sides of skillet to make a well in the middle; add 1 tsp. oil and crack eggs into the well. Add a spoonful of water, cover the skillet, and cook about 3 minutes more or to desired doneness. Sprinkle with cheese, tomato, and optional bacon bits before serving.

* *Reserved from Day 1 Dinner.*

** *Reserve remaining whole green beans for Day 3 Dinner.*

BBQ BACON RANCH DIP

Mix 1½ (8 oz.) pkgs. cream cheese (softened) and ½ C. prepared ranch dressing in a bowl; spread mixture in a pie pan. Spread with ⅓ C. BBQ sauce, ½ C. bacon bits, ½ C. diced bell pepper (any color), 1 diced tomato, and 1 C. shredded cheddar cheese. Chill at least 1 hour before serving with crackers or leftover hamburger buns (sliced, buttered, and toasted on the grill).

CHICKEN NOODLE SOUP
with Grilled Cheese

Butter

½ C. each chopped onion and celery

2 (14.5 oz.) cans chicken broth

1 to 1½ C. clear cooking liquid*

1 C. reserved shredded chicken*

1½ C. egg noodles

1 C. sliced raw carrots

½ tsp. each dried basil and oregano

Salt and black pepper to taste

8 bread slices

4 oz. cheddar cheese, sliced

1 tomato, sliced

In a medium saucepan over medium heat, melt 1 T. butter; sauté onion and celery until tender, about 5 minutes. Add broth, cooking liquid, chicken, noodles, carrots, and seasonings. Bring to a boil, then reduce heat and simmer about 20 minutes, until noodles and carrots are tender.

Meanwhile, butter one side of each bread slice. On four unbuttered sides, layer cheese and tomato slices. Top with remaining bread slices, buttered side up. Cook in a skillet over medium heat until golden brown on both sides.

* Use liquid and chicken reserved from Day 2 Dinner.

FLATBREAD PIZZAS
& Grilled Green Beans

Whole green beans*

1 T. olive oil

Salt and black pepper to taste

4 flatbread pizza crusts

Sauce: pizza sauce, ranch dressing, and/or BBQ sauce

Shredded cheese: cheddar, mozzarella, Parmesan

Bacon bits

Leftovers from your cooler: cooked chicken and roast beef, mushrooms, pepperoni, onions, tomatoes

* Reserved from Day 3 Breakfast

Trim beans and toss with oil, salt, and pepper. Set on a piece of foil *(crimp the edges)* on a grate over medium heat for 20 to 30 minutes, tossing occasionally, until crisp-tender and lightly browned. Meanwhile, set each crust on a large piece of greased foil and spread with desired sauce and toppings. Wrap foil loosely around pizzas and set on the grate over medium-low heat. Cook 5 to 10 minutes or until everything is hot and melty. Serve with green beans.

Try These Topping Combos

Chicken-Bacon-Ranch: *ranch dressing, chicken, green onion, bacon bits, mozzarella & Parmesan cheeses*

Meat-Lovers: *pizza or BBQ sauce, roast beef, pepperoni, mushrooms, tomato, bell pepper, onion & cheddar cheese*